"Don't Be Long Where You Don't Belong"

Written by: Christopher C. Smith

ISBN : 979-8-9893923-4-6

Christopher C. Smith

Father, Author, Actor, Song Writer, Independent Book & Movie Publisher

Thank you's & Dedications

First I would like to give thanks to God

My Beautiful Mother
Ora Henderson

My Beautiful Daughter
Lauren Madison Smith

My Supportive A.O.D Family

And everyone at store #5965
Pullman Chicago, Illinois

Sponsored By

Chapter 1

Hi, you've reached the voicemail...

Hi, you've reached Tony Iglesias. Sorry, I couldn't...

Huh? For some strange reason, I kept getting the voicemail when I tried to call.

While quickly getting dressed and putting on my shoes, I tried a couple more times, getting the same results each time.

I could only assume he was either busy or forgot to charge his phone, as he tends to do after having such a crazy night.

But as I thought to myself, there was no way I could go another minute without telling my only childhood friend, who had left since kindergarten, the amazing news.

I had just received news that I got my dream job, and I had finally picked out and purchased the engagement ring for my girl, which I had been saving up for over the past few years.

I could only imagine the look on his face when he saw the size of the rock and heard its price.

While speeding down the block, I couldn't help but notice the loud screaming and yelling, which sounded like a scene from one of those early '90s hood movies.

With little grass on the lawns and trash almost everywhere, I couldn't help but think that this might just be one of the scenes that was filmed out here.

As I drove closer and closer, only about a block away, I could see that it was the same couple who argued every other week about a bunch of irrelevant personal stuff that one would think should only be kept inside the house. After weaving through the small traffic and finally finding a parking space close to Tony's house, I screamed, "Ayooooo," in such an aggressive tone that only he knew it was me and hoped he could hear me.

"Aye...aye," I heard a light whisper. "Aye, aye."

With a paranoid look on my face, I began to look around to see where the voice was coming from.

As I looked to my left, I couldn't help but notice a short, older man trying to sell me something that looked like a small bag of weed.

This confused me for a moment, but as I thought about the good things I had going on, I started to ponder and think to myself, Hey, what the hell—there would be nothing wrong with a little celebration drug for once, knowing that I rarely even smoke or drink.

As he continued to try to get me to buy it, I eventually gave in.

Hey, what the heck?

And with that, the transaction was done, and for the first time in my life, I had purchased weed.

Knock, knock, knock...

Diiiiiiinnnggg Dooong! As I held my finger pressed hard on his doorbell, I knew it would make him very angry, lol.

As he finally came to the door, I could tell from his appearance and the reek of liquor on his breath that he had a crazy night.

"Yo, Tone, guess what just happened?" From the way I was yelling, he could tell I was hyped up and couldn't hold it in any longer.

"Guess what happened!"

"Wait, wait," he interrupted me, still yawning and wiping the sleep from his eyes.

He stood in front of the screen door, which looked as though it was due for an update soon, hanging on its last hinges.

"Come on in and calm down.

What's the hype about?" he said gently, with a smirk on his face as if he knew something was up.

"You'll never believe what I just did..."

Boom...boom!

As I started to sit down, I suddenly jumped in fear after hearing the loud noise at the door.

"Open up! I know you're in there!"

With a confused look on my face, I couldn't help but look at Tony as he began to yell, "Oh crap! Hurry up, let's head to the back—come on, come on!"

"Wait, what?" I asked. Without hesitation, I quickly followed his instructions and made my way to the back door.

Boom! The door we were heading toward was kicked in by what looked like the SWAT team.

"Put your hands up! Now lay on the ground! You guys are under arrest!"

"What's going on, Tony?" I yelled.

"You guys are under arrest. The chase is over.

I got you now!" one officer said while instructing more officers to come in and search throughout the house.

By the look on Tony's face, I couldn't help but notice that he seemed like he wanted to tell me something just as badly as I wanted to tell him.

But before I knew it, we were both in separate police cars, headed down to the Smithville Police Station.

Chapter 2

As we began to pull up in the parking lot of the police station, I still had such a shocked and confused look on my face as to what had just gone down.

"Wait right here," the officer said while getting out of the car and making his way around to get me from the rear passenger side.

I kept thinking, Is it me? Do I have a warrant or something?

I couldn't help but notice that as I made my way into the station, I took a quick glance to my left and saw Tony, cuffed to the bench, looking back at me with a "Hey, I'm sorry you had to go through this" type of stare.

While still feeling numb and in a daze, I heard the officer say, "Sit right next to him," as he insisted that I sit next to Tony and handcuffed my right hand to the bench.

"Don't say a word; I'll be right back."

"Hey, I'm sorry," Tony uttered under his breath, trying not to be heard.

"Wait, what happened? What's going on?

What in the world did you get me into?" I replied, as fear came over me and my voice began to crack.

From the look in Tony's eyes, it was clear he had done something serious or something bad was going to happen.

"Hey, look, this is what happened. About a week ago, I was low on cash and got introduced to a guy named Brandon from around the way."

"Wait, hold up," I interrupted, still trying not to be overheard.

"You do know that if you were low on money or needed quick cash, you could've come to me in the first place."

"I know, I know, but I... I didn't want to bother you or involve you in anything because you weren't that type of dude. But my gas had just been cut off, and I needed money to pay my child support since I had already fallen behind a few months.

I was afraid that after too long, the police would come and lock me up."

"I understand," I whispered back. "But finish the story. What just happened?"

"Okay, so look.

I met Brandon through another friend at a gas station where I was going to buy some drugs to flip.

But after Brandon dropped everything off and I let everyone know what I was doing and my plans to sell, I started making a lot of money.

For about a week, I was making so much that I got kind of greedy.

Before you knew it, I was calling Brandon back every other day for more and more drugs because people were blowing up my phone left and right."

"But for some strange reason, one lady in particular always walked by, staring at the line of people coming from the side of my house.

I figured she was up to something or had plans to snitch.

The last time I saw her, I said, 'Hey, what's up? What's going on?' and in a shocked, light tone, she warned me that some of the people she had seen at my house were informants and undercover cops.

She told me I needed to get out or stop as soon as possible."

"But the money was coming in so fast, it felt like a quick high.

I was getting addicted to every transaction I made."

"Wait, so hold up," I said, a frightened look on my face.

"This whole thing is a drug bust? We might be in serious trouble."

"It's crazy," I continued, "because I was coming over to tell you and show you the engagement ring I just bought for my girl."

While explaining the ring and its price, I noticed it was no longer in the pocket I had placed it in.

I started squirming and stood up.

"Hey! You, sit down now!" an officer yelled from across the room as I tried to explain about the ring and why I was looking for it.

"I'm not trying to hear that.

You should've thought about what you had done in the first place."

Still shocked and confused, I sat back down and asked Tony to continue.

I needed to know why I was in the police station, handcuffed to a bench.

"Listen, Zach.

I'm guessing they're doing a search at my house now as we speak."

"A search?" I replied.

"And in this search, what are they looking for?"

"Just listen," Tony said.

From his expression, I could tell he knew this was serious and that he might be facing jail time.

Smithville, USA, has some of the strictest drug and gun laws in the country.

"So, hear me out.

There were some drugs leftover and a gun or two I had hidden, just in case I got robbed or someone tried to mess with me."

"A gun?" I yelled, standing up as if that would draw even more attention to us.

"I warned you guys to shut up! Zach, I want you over here.

Tony, come with me now," the officer commanded.

As I looked at his badge, I noticed the name said Officer Thompson.

For some reason, it rang a bell as if I knew him.

As Officer Thompson walked Tony away, I heard the front door of the station swing open.

Officers were carrying large, black, heavy garbage bags.

"Yeah, we got them now!" one officer shouted, clearly excited.

From the tone of his voice, I could only hope to God that the bags weren't from Tony's house.

When I looked at Tony, his expression told me he was feeling worse and worse as the minutes passed.

"Excuse me, officer," I whispered to the young lady behind the desk.

"Do you have any idea what's going on?"

She replied, "No, not really, but I'm sure you guys will get a phone call before the fingerprinting and everything."

As she spoke, my face lit up slightly.

It didn't really matter what else she said; I was focused on that one statement about the phone call.

Interrupting her, I asked, "Sorry, but when do we get this phone call?"

"Look, I know I'm not supposed to do this now, and I could get in trouble, but give me the number, and I'll call for you."

As she dialed the number, I heard someone pick up on the first ring.

It sounded like my fiancée.

"Hello? Hello?"

I could tell by the tone of her voice that she was just as shocked to get the call as I was to be in that situation.

"Hey, I have Zach here, and he wants to talk to you quickly and explain what's going on."

"Hey, bae," I said.

"Umm, what's going on, Zach? Are you okay?"

"Well, sort of no," I said, as I broke down and explained to Angie what had happened with the raid and why I was at the station.

"But what about tonight and the plans we had?" she asked.

I could tell by her voice that she was upset and on the verge of tears.

It hit me hard because today was the day I planned to propose—our anniversary.

We had plans to eat dinner at the same place where we first met.

"I'm so sorry," I said.

Just then, an officer approached. I quickly hung up the phone as he uncuffed me and walked me to the back to be fingerprinted and placed in the interrogation room, just like in those TV shows and movies.

Chapter 3

"Order in the court!"

The judge yelled at the top of his lungs while slamming the gavel a few times, and before you knew it, the court was silent.

"Wow," I thought as I stared slowly around the courtroom.

I couldn't believe I had spent my weekend in a terrible holding cell with thin mattresses, balled up in the corner while using my shirt to stretch over my whole body.

While continuing to look around, I noticed some familiar faces besides those of my family.

But one face in particular I couldn't help but notice was absent—my girl. With my hands cuffed behind me, I held my head down until the judge spoke.

"Will Anthony Iglesias and Zack please come to the front?"

As I began to walk in front of the judge, I started to feel more and more butterflies.

The closer I got, the more nervous I became.

With Tony standing beside me, I couldn't help but notice the sadness and disappointment in his stare.

"So, Anthony," the judge said in such an angry voice as if he knew him personally and was fed up with the whole situation.

"What did you think was going to happen?

Knowing that you were already on parole, and then deciding to miss a couple of court dates for the type of case you have going on.

Please, sir, look at me while I'm speaking to you.

Give me one good reason why I shouldn't throw the book at you this time around."

As the judge began to list all the infractions that had put us in this position, I couldn't help but think that Tony hadn't been 100% honest with me when he told me everything that was going on.

The more I heard the judge speaking, the more furious I became as to why I was even tied to this mess.

"Sorry, sir, I definitely apologize," Tony said in a light voice as he started to answer the judge's question.

My facial expression became duller as I realized this was a very serious situation, and we were about to go down hard.

With him accumulating warrant after warrant and the evidence they found during the raid, you could tell by the tension between the judge and Tony that everything was going downhill.

While looking at both of our public defenders, I started to wonder, "When are they going to say something in our defense?"

Feeling quite disgusted by their blank stares, I couldn't help but think they were only there for show and not genuinely interested in defending us.

With a slightly aggressive tone, I interrupted the judge, "Excuse me, Your Honor," I said, cutting off his conversation with Tony.

"Quiet!" he said while slamming the gavel again, this time even harder.

He began to read from what seemed like a stack of papers that the officers had handed him.

"For you, Zack," the judge yelled as he locked eyes with me, speaking in an aggressive tone, "you knew what your charges were, correct?"

I swallowed hard enough to hear and then replied, "Yes, sir, I am aware that conspiracy to distribute is a very serious crime."

But in my mind, I refused to let my homie, whom I knew since we were kids, go down like this.

While being asked interrogating questions, I kept my mouth shut, refusing to snitch.

The judge carried on, and I held my head down as he began to read my charges.

The main one was conspiracy and something else I couldn't quite make out, along with the time I would be serving: 52 months.

"52 months!" I yelled.

"Quiet!" he replied. As my knees began to collapse and go numb, I whispered to my public defender, "How many years is that?"

"A little over four years," he replied. "But look at it like this, you only have to do 85% of the time, then you'll be eligible for parole."

I gave him a smirk, thinking, "Really? Come on now."

I couldn't be too mad, though, because it did beat having to serve the whole sentence.

But still—wow—I thought to myself.

The judge then turned to Tony and began to read off his charges and what he would be sentenced to, which totaled around 86 months due to being on the run, accumulating warrants for not showing up, and the evidence found during the raid.

There were also a few witnesses who stood up and provided statements about the drug operation he had going on at his house, which brought even more attention to himself.

Looking around the room to see who was present, I saw Tony lock eyes with what appeared to be a familiar face.

I heard him whisper under his breath, "Not you again," only to find out that the lady who had warned him earlier about the attention he was drawing was actually one of the witnesses.

She had written statements and had been spying on him, along with the guy who sold me the weed.

As we both held our heads down while being carried away, I couldn't help but think about how the job I had just gotten and the chance to be engaged were now out the window.

I might not get another chance at all to find a great job with a bad record or to find the love of my life.

But I was more worried about Tony, who looked exhausted and defeated.

"Hey, you okay?" I whispered.

"I got your back, my dude.

We're in this together.

They might have our bodies here, but they don't have our minds and souls."

While speaking and trying to motivate him, I could tell it brought some light to him as he wiped the tears from his eyes.

"Wow, four years," I said, shaking my head in disbelief.

I still couldn't believe this was how I was going out.

I would have never thought in a million years that I would end up in this situation.

"This has got to be a part of God's plan,"

I thought as I walked to my cell and began to pray for guidance and strength to walk down the long road ahead of me.

Chapter 4

As I sat up on my bed while staring at the wall, I couldn't help but break down as tears started to fill my eyes, and my chest began to tighten up.

Thinking, Wow, two and a half years have really gone by.

"I can't believe this," I cried.

"My life is over.

I'm done!"

"Hey, calm down.

It could be a lot worse, kiddo, chill out."

As I started to turn my head in the direction from which I heard the voice, what seemed like a pretty woman appeared.

To my surprise, with a shocked look on my face, I couldn't believe it.

It was, in fact, the secretary who, when I first came in, let me use the phone to make the call to my girl.

"Hey, what are you doing here?" I asked as I made my way to the cell bars. "Aren't you…"

"Shhh," she interrupted. "I am who you think I am, but I wanted to help you.

I got word on what happened to you guys,

which I think is pretty messed up—how it was all a setup."

"Yes, it is messed up.

I can't believe my life is in shambles now," I said, my voice cracking as I began to cry again, my head hanging low between the cell bars.

"Look, hear me out.

I have a plan," she suggested.

"A plan? What do you mean? A plan?"

"Yes, a plan—to get you out of here.

Then, we go to where your friend is and get him out too, and we all make a run for the border.

So, are you down or not?"

I took a deep breath and thought to myself, Hey, why not?

I've hit rock bottom and have nothing to lose or live for anymore.

But the harder I thought about her and the plan and how we were going to get out, it hit me.

I looked at her with the strangest look before asking, "Um, and what is your name again?"

She giggled before replying, "Sooo, you used my phone to call another female without even asking my name?"

While thinking to myself, I couldn't help but admit she had a point.

Before I knew it, I asked, "So, umm, what is your first and last name, if you don't mind me asking?"

After locking eyes for a second or two, we both began to laugh out loud.

"Well, hi, my name is Jenny."

"Oh, okay," I replied in a sarcastic tone. "You do look like a Jenny Johnson, I must add."

"Oh, so you got jokes, I see," she said as she began to show me some drawings and small notes she had jotted down on what looked like crumpled construction papers detailing how we were going to sneak out of here.

While reading and still asking questions, one big issue that really crossed my mind was the barbed wires that were tied around the fences and the alarm sounds that would activate if someone crossed certain lines.

But with each question I asked, Jenny had all the answers as if she was some sort of professional at successfully getting people out of here.

I took a deep breath and agreed, trying not to draw any attention to myself.

We agreed to start with the first step on the list:

to be up and ready to go at 3 a.m. Watching her walk off as if nothing happened, I started to pace back and forth, feeling more nervous than ever as my palms began to sweat.

God, I can't believe I'm doing this, I thought to myself, just thinking of the risk I was taking.

I had never been this scared in my life until the time came to execute the plan. Moment by moment, bit by bit, I won't lie—I was full of anxiety and adrenaline as each step of the plan was being carried out exactly as Jenny had planned.

I could see myself, for some reason, catching feelings for her.

"Hey, are you okay?"

she asked softly but loud enough for me to hear.

As the sun began to rise, the more we progressed, the more I could feel freedom was underway.

Still, I couldn't deny that this journey was making me feel like she was sent by God himself or some kind of guardian angel, considering how everything had come about.

"Hey, watch your step.

This is the final one," she said as I spotted headlights not too far ahead.

They belonged to a friend of hers or something like that, waiting for us.

While trying to keep up with her as we got closer, I couldn't help but grab her by the hand, turning her around to lock eyes with her and finally give her a long kiss. She gently kissed me back.

"Thank you for everything,"

I whispered.

"Oh wow, no prob.

I was wondering when you were going to make that move, Zack.

Looks like it came sooner than later."

As we made our way down the road, undressing and changing into the clothes that were in the back seat of the car,

I could only think about my homie who was locked up not too far away and what his reaction would be when he saw us as we planned our great escape across the border to be free once again.

"How are you feeling?" she asked.

"By the way, Shawn, this is my friend Zack. Zack, this is Shawn."

As Jenny introduced us, I felt like I knew him from somewhere, but I couldn't quite put my finger on it.

I just nodded and laid back as we pulled up to a gas station about 40 miles away.

I assumed we were stopping to fill up and grab some snacks.

"Hey," Jenny said, "I'm going in here. You just lay back or rest for a bit so no one sees or recognizes you while I go pay and pump the gas."

Without arguing, I did just that. I twisted, turned, and lay in every position possible.

As hard as it was, I couldn't fall asleep as my mind raced, thinking about how I really escaped.

"So, tell me more about yourself, Jen," I asked, hoping to start a conversation and get to know her more.

As time went on and we exchanged life stories and what we had been through, I could tell by the overwhelming look on her face that we had a lot in common.

"Hey, how much longer until we get to where Tony is?" I asked.

"Not far," Shawn and Jenny replied at the same time.

But how would he know where to go or what to do?

I thought to myself but soon after asked Jenny. She replied, "He knows we're coming, and the guards and I are cool.

They're aware of what's going on, so he should be waiting for us by the gates.

He was instructed to change clothes because he was given a guard's uniform, so those who don't know what's going on won't pay much attention to him."

As the conversation grew and the day went on, I could see from the expressway that we weren't too far from the location.

Sitting in silence, I realized I hadn't eaten in almost a day due to overthinking how things would pan out.

Seconds later, my stomach let out a loud growl as a reminder that if I didn't get something soon, I would pass out.

"Wow," Jenny turned around as Shawn laughed out loud.

"What was that?" she asked, giggling.

I turned my head to stare out the window in embarrassment.

"I'm starving," I admitted.

"Well, look, there's a Smitty Burger Joint inside the Smith Mart a couple of miles ahead," Shawn suggested.

"Well, hurry up, I'm not sure how much longer I can take."

Within minutes, we pulled up to the window.

As Jenny placed the order, I couldn't help but notice the clerk at the window being quite nosy, trying to look inside the car as if we looked familiar.

"Hey, you're Zack, right? And you're Jennifer?"

With a shocking look on all of our faces, we all asked at the same time, "What's wrong? How did you know?"

"Well, look," the clerk said, pointing to the TV screen through the window.

Sure enough, it read: Missing inmate Zack Miller and inmate employee Jennifer reported missing.

If anyone has seen them, please call authorities as they are considered armed and dangerous.

Just reading it alone made my heart drop, and everything in my body felt like it hit the floor.

Feeling stuck, I looked around to make sure no one else noticed us.

We quickly paid for our food and sped off.

"In three miles, make a left on Smithville Blvd," the GPS spoke gently.

I started to feel some relief knowing that soon I would be back with my homie and we could ride out and get away from all this craziness.

"How are you guys feeling?" I asked.

After taking a deep breath, they both replied, "Relieved."

As we got closer to the destination, I could see Tony ahead, dressed up and trying not to look too suspicious.

"Yo, hey, you!" I yelled with my window half-cracked.

He jumped into the car, and we were on our way!

Chapter 5

Wow, looking at my homie in amazement, I couldn't help but think that just a week ago, we were both locked up and probably never going to see each other again.

"Aye, did you see this?" Tony asked as he passed me the phone.

To my shock, it was the same girl in a picture with one of the officers who had raided the place.

The officer was proposing to her with the ring I had bought, and I was on my way to Tony's house to show him.

As I stood there with a completely blank look on my face, I couldn't help but stare and say in a low voice, "Wow." To think that, in Tony's eyes, it was just my girl being proposed to by the officer in the raid.

"Man," I said as I felt my heart drop and my stomach fold four times over.

Without wanting to speak or explain anything, I quickly handed Tony back the phone and stared out the window.

At that very moment, I was torn apart completely and felt as low as I possibly had in my entire life.

"Hey, you guys ready to start a new life?" Jenn said excitedly.

She didn't even know what was going on.

I simply nodded my head yes, without showing that I had started shedding tears.

The End

www.ingramcontent.com/pod-product-compliance
Lightning Source LLC
Chambersburg PA
CBHW071932020426
42331CB00010B/2825